Newbridge Hill

Trodden leaf on the street, you fell nearby
Brown, Red and yellow, never lurid, always subtle
pushed aside under inept feet
Feet that have forgotten where they came from.
You have always known, but it is always the
wise that are stepped on.
These feet lost their way three moons ago
caring nothing for street leaves, such as you.
They have only time for pretty things,
A blossom tree in full bloom perhaps
but not you. You , who do not make a spectacle
and yet have so much to give.
If only they would look for you!
Your death, a slow process, breaks my heart.
You came and went without words,
without airs and graces.
Inept feet quashed you en route to the Taj Mahal
to remove their shoes in reverence.
A piece of you rests now in the boot rack-
golden slumber beneath the dirt.
More will come of course,
they always do
But you- you were here once for a while
And I hope you know I noticed you.

Night, in Hiding

Sometimes the sky is wiped quite bare
barren stretch, no chance to stare
at natures night, although still there
shall tonight remain in hiding

A poets mind this night denied
her muse enchantress; wont provide
the majestic stars so oft her guide
shall tonight remain in hiding

And though this eve she is alone
abandoned by the great unknown
she's never , really, on her own
with tomorrows stars to guide her.

Universe

Universe; your beauty

Enthrals and consumes me.

Who are you? What are you trying to say?

I'm not sure we will ever figure you out

I am so grateful

You comfort me when there is no-one else

Just one look and things make sense;

Sense from the unknown

Makes no sense!

My senses are overwhelmed by you

universe,

I trust you, you will never leave me

My best friend when

There is no-one else.

I had some-one once,

he knew you too

But he is gone now,

to consume you alone

Without me.

In Memory

Am I looking at her now?

As I'm sitting here tonight.

Is she around here somewhere,

Is she hiding, out of sight.

Is she there, amongst the branches

Is she sprinkled 'cross the sky

Is she somehow caught on earth still

As she tries to say goodbye.

And I always shall remember

(though we only spoke awhile)

her beauty, brains and kindness

wisdom, charm and smile

And I thought they would have noticed

And I would have thought they'd care

Their beginning was her ending,

and it just seems so unfair.

Is she listening to my memory

Does she know how I recall

the impact that she had on me

as I was about to fall.

And although I'll never tell her

just how her death changed me

I think perhaps, shes everywhere;

in memory, she is free.

Them

How do they do it?

The ones with the smiles

They make it seem so easy

yet I have walked for miles

and still cannot work it out.

No solution to that which is easy

for them.

They are lucky, What I would give!

To not question, analyse and die

One death a day. [Sometimes more]

Dramatic is my middle name,

Ironic too, I failed at acting.

Do they act?

The ones with the smiles?

I dont believe they do. Its natural

I'm not so different, I'm just the same

Perhaps I dont want to be

like them.

February

Calm grey light of the evening

Slowly breathing, silently being,

Barely moving, yet so alive.

Natures shadows prominent;

Against the starless sky.

A timeless scene,

Tranquillity, broken by birdsong.

Continual life,

Majestic life,

Centuries old and still breathing!

Flickers, synthetic, far off..

Humanity in self destruct,

Forgetting the gooses cry.

For now the starless sky remains,

Until false light consumes the world.

A lesson

The moon is low

casually drifting t'ward earth

time taken, peacefully reaching the end.

Beyond the pines, he glimmers,

politely through;

a small beam beneath

the flickers over head.

He does not fear an end,

neither does he complain

Only lingers, quietly.

Until he plays his part in the day;

(casting shadows across the land)

until tomorrow, as once again

the universe calls upon him.

Musings on loss

Its something that I heard them say,

"Why did you have to go away?"

"to where?" they say, "and how, and why?"

for what reasons did he die?

Some even say; he's not gone far-

his smile is in the nearest star

and when you are alone, they swear

you'll hear his whispers in the air.

He's hiding in the fallen leaves,

(even if no-one believes)

They'll feel and know his precense yet:

neither can nor will forget.

So in the silence of your night

within that darkness, there is light.

Its just something that I heard them say;

he'll never really go away.

Snow

Exquisite white melody
icy notes fall low
Each in its own excellence
In rhythm and in flow
Briefly lingered lyrics
Ephemeral glow
Then silently melting
As all beauty must go.

A love poem to Nature

Ethereal Beauty
I am rendered speechless
In your presence
Infinities complexion;
A blushing landscape
A graceful surrender
Your smile stirs
My very existence
And to think;
At any moment you could be gone.

Ponderings

I sit

Where glass panes let souls fly
where imaginations run
and do not lie
emptily in their beds
but join the planets
orbiting hell

and up

and up
up

and up some more
a speck of dust in
an attic
a fleck of paint
on dark canvas
A something in infinity
fleeting

flickering
floating

for who? for what?
and why does it stay?

I sit
and ponder
Until its time to close the window for the day.

The Sleep Thief [1]

Sleep is a thief

With a coat of luring rainbow colours

To entrance you to his lair

Inside the lining, the coat is the blackest of blacks

Enough to swallow hopes and dreams

Oh yes, he gives dreams too

But they are the dreams of sleep

They are false and alluring

Sleeps trick to keep you to himself

He steals dreams of life that

Are so clear at the days end

At dawn, like the stars, they have disappeared

And who has taken them?

It was sleep. Untrustworthy sleep

I will never rest again.

The Sleep thief's return

He's here again

Stark figure against the lamplight
He's come for you
Everyday the same, escape impossible
You cannot live without him
You need him as much as air
And yet he takes and
Only gives illusions back.
Leaves you with a
bittersweet taste of success
Short-lived, reality hits in
The morning light. Cruel and fresh
Against the prospects of the day;
Lack of, says you, for he
Has taken everything
The night before. Now you
Start again to build the purpose
And the dreams you want to have;
When sleep stops stealing
dreams away.

The Sleep Thief [3]

Cloaked figure sing your praises
Raise your banner high
For you have won again
The stampede of wonder reigned
Once more in the dark hours
Pale anguish of the day, why are
You here. If it were not for him
You would be different. You bastard
You have brought the ache, the
Wolves that tear me open and snatch
Away my earnings. Thieves, thieves
Thieves. Not one alone but several
scheming toads, they live in swamps
and hang their cloaks on stolen wings
from little girls who dared to dream
deepest realms of evil. Sing your praises
raise your banner high
for you have won again.

Everything

Every rock and every stream,
Every drop of rain falls gleam;
stands apart from any other-
mother, father, sister, brother.
Every sand speck of the shore
Every seagulls lament, or
a singular soul in his own right
a timeless, enduring beautiful sight.
Every note of every tune
Every body gone too soon
So alive!, sleeps in the air
so exposed to those aware
Every tale, every romance
Every song and every dance
there lies a thing to most unknown
some exquisite sense that I call home.

Fireflies

I saw two stars playing

tag; Nimbly darting to and fro

Across the sky, the leapt,

They danced,

But were they stars?

I do not know.

The goodbye Letter

It isnt that I need you here-

Or even if I do,

It doesnt make a difference;

Theres no more me and you.

Its not to do with romance-

I love you as a friend

So why cant I shake the feeling

this shouldnt be the end.

And I know that things are different,

I know I should not care

its just that despite everything

sometimes I need you there

So I'll see this as a parting

(although I wish that I knew why)

your beginning is our endin g

And I must mean goodbye.

All that has passed

I'm caught in a spell of their making,

little wisps of a dream from

the night before.

I'm staring across misty hours,

and finding their songs

are unheard now.

And there she is again..

quite silent, their tales

are collected in her eyes

(even as we are speaking)

I'm not sure I could say why

these pieces have drifted so;

across time

Never to be beautiful

To all.

Who is there to remember
you but me?
Oh sure, many speak
of you from time to time
perhaps even write
a poem
sing a song;
or two
but who will remember
you?
Perhaps a mourner who,
at that time of
great despair
vowed never have
a single care
again, and now
the years are passed
his vow of course
could never last
And you are dead-
still gone away.
I'll think of you
but every day.
You dont know me;
I dont know you
(nor ever shall) but
still its true
I'll think of you
: to all of you.

Grounded

I have a dream but
That word is overrated so
I have a hope,
A desire,
A delusion,
It's a secret, I cant say
Only leads to more dismay
Dare to dream?
Ah! But why? To
Build and build, never
To fly? Why not
Stay grounded
And never try.

Wednesday 17th, 11.45pm

I long to lie on icy ground
crystal blades digging in my back
to gaze at the world from
my place in it, right now
no waiting around
its all here in this moment
on this freezing grass bed
I would stare and stare
clouds of air rising
from gasps of awe
frozen completely, yet
would not if I could
move; held in overwhelming
bemusement at the wonder of it all
This surely is, in this moment
what its all about.

May

Water-coloured earth
stretched o'er pale land
streaming ribbons in the wind
Forest knitting skylight blue,
Cornflowers splashed white
Visually feasting
lightning bug smiles
Yonder-eyed pixies
gingerly peeping through
high willow thistles
brushed gently in melody.
This is May,
As birdsong kissed stream
to nymphal lair flows.

For a Magic World

Do you think the sun would fail to rise
if unicorns flew in sapphire skies?

Do you think the moon would hide away
If elves and imps came out to play?

Could you accept that they were there
if mermaids swam in salty air?

Would you accept that it were true
If fairies came to call for you?

And would you leave your world behind
to risk another realm of mind?
And put all you have and all you know
aside, and let reality go.

Do you think the world would cease to be
If magic existed readily?

If only man could comprehend!
without mystery the world will end.

Snowdrop

White ocean wild,
sweeping wooded blanket
carpetted softly
the faeries den.
Petticoat sprinklings
'cross fen and spring
snow velvet petals
pure to taste
januarys awakening.
Nestled shy, heads low
melting in forest floor
Delicate canopies
in winters last blizzard.

Bluebells

Along the dirt track
beyond the nettle forest
into the undergrowth
past the rotting leaves
they await
a carpet of blue
enchanting, bewitching
a childhoods dream
it sings to you
a feast for the eyes
and moreso, the imagination
comes alive at every flower
a fairys 'achoo!'
hiding amongst the petals as
her dust, twinkling, fills the
air. Clear innocence
beauty of the soul,
naivety of the mind
the blue carpet will line
my mind forever.

Ecstasy

What drug is this?

What warm engulfment
What all-encompassing sensation
I breathe in
surrounded and intoxicated
in this power
Like drowning; life
flashes by
Forgotten senses, lost
in childhoods slumber
I breathe in wood smoke,
a darkened house against
the sunken skyline
Overwhelming dusk
Breathes memories
I had thought lost in fumes
What bewitchment
nature supplies.

Untitled

Write me tales

of life and lust

of truths, and dreams

and fairy dust

I want to hear,

I want to see,

I want so deeply

to be free

And all I know

from lifetimes song

I'd love so madly

to belong

I'm caught between

the now and then,

perhaps I could

begin again?

I'm all a-swim

its all a mess

high expectations

no more, no less.

So come with me

lets float away

We'll start this year

Another day

I saw the Moon

I turned to see the moon
As so many have before
I turned to see
A slice of past
And I noticed the future
was hiding in the shadows.
Waiting.
I turned to see
everything thats real
everything
safe, within
illumination
I turned to see
humanity
transforming
as the moons face
shys in the darkness
And yet,

as I turn

a calm

timelessness emblazons
the night sky.

I turned to see the moon
I'll always see the moon.

Tomorrows dreamer

Moonlight thinker
hold your breath
open souled
for evenings death
Starlight dancer
strike a pose
leaping barefoot
through your woes
Nighttime dreamer
do not fear
your hope and stars
are ever near
Oh, Moonlight thinker
weave your way
cast dreams and spells
upon the day.

What is going on?

Oh just what is going on?
Does anybody know?
If someone finds the answer
oh just tell me where to go

Oh just what is going on?
Would someone like to tell?
I'm dying just to be informed
we're fine and all is well

Oh just what is going on?
The grounds gone beneath my feet
I'm searching hard for something
but that somethings incomplete

Oh just what is going on?
Would someone care to share?
As everybody seems to know
yet I'm so unaware

Oh just what is going on?
Oh, you say you're searching too?
Then tell, at least, just how
the act comes easily to you!

Oh just what is going on?
its impossible to find!
but the fact we're all oblivious
provides some peace of mind

Oh just what is going on?
for now my quest complete
even with the answers missing
the world is at my feet.

Poison

Magic colour your
possibilities amaze me.
Endless energy, sight
and sound fill my head
with terrifying excitement.
Addictive and charming
in nature, it lures me in.
One moment is all it takes
to fill the room with
wonder. I want to stay
like this forever! Another?
[Normalities gone of course].
How wonderful this colour is,
even the ceiling enchants me;
another sip is all it takes
to reach infinity. Is this allowed
or is it all an act to
escape from a reality?
Maybe.

"Shorts"

#1 Nightwords

Sometimes I wake in the night,

with an intense desire to write

I'll kick of the sheet

and get to my feet

to find not one pen in sight!

#2 Write

Pen in mouth

sharp against teeth

plastic bitten; bittersweet

Comforting habit

perhaps uncouth

taking dark dreams

replacing with truth

3 Nightmare

Tonight I'll sleep to tarnished hopes

or casualties of swinging rope

But in the morn

for whence I wake

that tragedy the day shall take.

4 The tree Imp

If my life were up to me

I would live in a hollowed tree

where I am oh so hard to see

and all the mice look up to me

Perhaps the squirells would feed me

with acorns and berries from the tree

and even though its cold I see

that this is just so right for me

Colour the World

Fill my world with colour,

Fill my soul with sound

and dont look back into the gloom

A cacophony of jewels

litter my mind - but briefly so

Please stay pretty ones,

your precense is inspiring!

Fireflies in the summer light

I am surrounded by magic.

A heavy anticipation hangs in balance

thick with promise;

I only fear eruption;

Shards of glass to pierce the heart

Dont hurt me please,

just fill my world with colour.

brilliant and magic

like heavy summer air.

Printed in Great Britain
by Amazon.co.uk, Ltd.,
Marston Gate.